WE DON'T DO "JUST OKAY" ANYMORE

by Susan Padron

Published by

Read Furiously

Read Often. Read Well.

Published by Read Furiously. First Edition.

ISBN: 978-1-7371758-0-3

Essays
Style/Fashion
Women Empowerment
Spirituality

A version of A Mother's Tale During COVID was originally published in Furious Lit vol 1: Tell me a story.

For more information on *We don't do "just okay" anymore* or Read Furiously, please visit readfuriously.com. For inquiries, please contact samantha@readfuriously.com.

Edited by Samantha Atzeni
Photo cover by: Jessica Lynn

Read (v): The act of interpreting and understanding the written word.

Furiously (adv): To engage in an activity with passion and excitement.

Read Often. Read Well. Read Furiously

TABLE OF CONTENTS

INTUITION

SHADOW SIDE

TRANSFORMATION

Intuition: your inner knowing, a gut instinct/feeling

Shadow Side: the emotional part of you that needs work, where you need to dig deep and do the hard stuff

Transformation: an evolution, an arrival

INTUITION

INTRO: UNSOLISITED ADVICE ABOUT LIFE AND STYLE

Intuition Intuition Intuition Intuition Intuition Intuition

On June 21, 2017, I left Hamilton as a middle school music teacher for the last time. I said my silent goodbyes to the building and the district, and had emotional goodbyes with my coworkers that had become family. But despite the sadness I felt leaving my friends, I finally felt at peace.

When I walked out of the building, I remember my ability to breathe changed – it actually became lighter and easier. I felt my energy quieten and remained that way for more than a few minutes at a time. I had been a middle school music teacher for seven years, and as scary as it is to leave a profession, everything in my body knew it was what I needed to do.

My final week teaching, I spent a lot of time thinking about everything that I learned about myself since becoming a teacher. The students taught me that I have more patience than I ever thought possible. I learned that I am a full-on mama bear when it comes to protecting and defending the people I care about, even my former students. Teaching middle school band unexpectedly prepared me for public speaking. I am frequently asked if I get nervous before I stand in front of an audience to facilitate a workshop or host a talk. Honestly, I am always excited, but if I can handle speaking in front of a room of middle school students with instruments in their hands, I can handle any group of adults.

My students also taught me that children are stronger than

you think, and it's impressive and heartbreaking at the same time. Teaching in Hamilton, you hear so many - too many - stories about the awful home lives that these kids have, and for some of them, you would never know because they are polite rays of sunshine. No matter what, you just hope for the best.

It wasn't until years after I left teaching that I learned that I am an empath. Being an empath means that you are able to feel the emotions of others, as though their emotions are your own. Kind of when you ask your friend how she's doing, and she responds with "fine;" you know she's not really fine. Empaths know that she's not fine before they even ask because by being in the same room as her, they - the empath- all of a sudden don't feel fine either. I remember that there were more days than I could count, where I would come home feeling emotionally drained for "no apparent reason," or I would experience emotions that I couldn't pinpoint their origins.

When you don't know that you're an empath, the constant, immediate absorption of other people's emotions can be tough. When you don't know that you're an empath, and you're around young people, who are on an emotional roller coaster, (middle school, remember?) and those same young people have really tough stories, you become an unwilling participant on their roller coaster. Thankfully, I have met wonderful people in my life on my spiritual journey that have taught me how to understand the gifts of being an empath, while also showing me how to protect and cleanse my own energetic body, so I am no longer an emotional sponge.

◖

I don't really know what changed to make me decide to leave teaching. I don't think it was one specific event or reason. I give my all to everything I am passionate about, and I knew it wasn't fair to my coworkers or my students to stay if I couldn't give 100%

anymore.

I do, however remember the exact time my priorities shifted, and it started with an asshole supervisor. Oh, asshole supervisors. They truly are a gift, am I right?

After teaching for three years in one middle school, I made the decision to transfer so I could have the opportunity to co-teach with another music teacher in our district. His former co-teacher was retiring, and he reached out to me about working together. I was honored, and I jumped on the chance. (Not the asshole part).

This same school year, our district got a new music supervisor (enter the asshole). He had been a music teacher in a very wealthy district, and made the decision to get his supervisor certification for the salary increase (fine, no judgement there, but he's still an asshole for later reasons).

Every school year, all of the middle school music groups put on a winter concert in December and a spring concert in May. In order to continue to grow the band program, we start beginners in sixth grade. By beginners, I mean, students who have never touched a musical instrument before in their lives. They have to learn how to read music, play an instrument, and learn how to play 2-3 songs from September to their winter concert in December... all while only having band class every other day in a group lesson format. It's not ideal by any means, but you make it work.

Okay, so why is this supervisor an asshole? The winter concert happened, and all of the bands performed, including the band of all beginners. Was it rough? Of course it was. But was it also really wonderful that these kids are finding a new way to express themselves and their creativity, and they're able to show that off to their families? Abso-fuckin-lutely.

My new (asshole) supervisor attended about ten minutes of each winter concert to show his support, which we appreciated. Our former supervisor did not always attend; in fact, he rarely showed up, but this is not about him. A week or so after my concert, our asshole supervisor attended one of the other middle school band concerts. My former colleague/work wife and current bestie, Mandy, the vocal music director was chatting with our supervisor. The Asshole Supervisor asked Mandy if she wanted to hear something funny. She, being the always polite human that she was and still is, obliged him, and he played her a recording on his phone. It was a recording of the beginner band from my concert. And then he began to say all kinds of awful things about their performance. And THEN he said how he, *along with the band directors from the other middle schools*, all had a good laugh at this recording when they went out for drinks together.

At this point, you might be thinking, "Wait, Susan left teaching because her supervisor said rude things about her to her friend?" Let me stop you there. You don't know me yet, and that's okay. Hopefully as you keep reading, you'll know me better.

Mandy told me what happened with our asshole supervisor, and I was furious. I am a mama bear through and through, and you don't fuck with my kids. At this point in my life, my kids were my students. I can handle criticism, especially constructive criticism. What made me so furious about this entire situation was that my asshole supervisor didn't talk to me about my program. Instead, he recorded a portion of my program, with the sole purpose of mocking my students as an attempt to bond with the other music teachers.

After talking with Mandy, I gathered the facts, tamed my emotions a bit, and went right to my principal. My principal was livid - the new supervisor was talking shit on one of *his* teachers in *his* music program at *his* school. The Asshole's boss, the assistant superintendent, was contacted and after that, my principal, Asshole Supervisor, and I all had a meeting.

◗

I may have been a 5'2", late 20something woman, most likely in an adorably stylish outfit, but you better believe I had "do NOT fuck with me" written all over my forehead at that meeting.

The Asshole Supervisor looked like a train wreck - beyond like a dog with his tail between his legs.

But nothing really changed after that meeting. Well, that's not entirely true. The Asshole Supervisor did everything in his power to avoid direct contact with me from that point forward.

The Asshole Supervisor's punishment ended up being more of a slap on the wrist. He continued to go out drinking with the other band directors, continued to say things about me and my program (that would occasionally get back to me), and I continued to do my job.

That whole experience allowed me to shift my priorities. My job was no longer my life. Allowing myself to be so wounded on behalf of my students and my program, when there weren't any real consequences for his actions, just seemed unnecessary. This was the first time I was able to start to step away from teaching.

I also knew I was finally ready to become a mom. My first class of sixth graders that I had for all three years, before sending them off to high school, showed me that I was meant to be one. And just days after officially resigning from teaching, I was able to watch many of them graduate from high school. Because I was a teacher, I knew that I was meant to be a mom, and I am grateful for that.

So, what happened after I left teaching?

I turned my side hustle of personal styling into my full time styling career.

I am grateful that a community of entrepreneurs has evolved because there is no way that I would have made it through the first year without them. As great as my college experience was, there was never a time when someone said, "Let me tell you what happens when you decide to change careers." If the topic of job change was discussed, it was still career adjacent - instead of teaching middle school band, you could teach high school band, or perform professionally with your own private teaching studio, or there's always grad school! I hope you can see me rolling my eyes to those options.

At the very beginning, when I started my business, I created a blog, so I could have an online presence in addition to social media. Somehow I found the Philadelphia blogging community, and that's how I made my first entrepreneur friends. Through the connections I made in that group and others, I have been able to find my tribe of amazing support. Being an entrepreneur can be lonely because you are everything to your business in the beginning. It is beyond crucial to find people in your life that have been where you are. Your family and friends are great, but you need people who understand, because they've been through it too. Not only can they offer advice, but they can provide you with resources and practical guidance.

So that's what I'm here for in this book. I'm here to offer you unsolicited advice based on my experience. Of course we'll talk about style and fashion, because I'm a stylist, and that's probably a big reason why you wanted to read this book in the first place.

You'll also get a bit of emotional support that may encourage you to look inward, but the beauty of a book is that if it gets to be too much for you, set it down, and come back to it when the time is right.

If you're ready now, let's get into it!

Intuition Intuition Intuition Intuition Intuition Intuition

HOW DO YOU WANT TO BE SEEN: WHO AM I?

Time for some tough love. I'm just going to get right to it. My clients are constantly struggling with being seen and heard. I believe that this is something that has become a problem due to other people, regardless of gender, making judgements on who we are, before we even start a conversation. It's easy to make negative initial assumptions about people, because it can be a way to protect ourselves from making any new connections in life. But, what if people made a positive assumption about you instead? Scarier yet, what if that assumption was right?

> Fashion can be a very powerful tool. Don't underestimate it, and don't sell yourself short.

I can't even begin to tell you how often I hear from clients over the age of 40, who say things like, "I'm invisible," and "No one sees me." It's heartbreaking. I know that my younger clients feel this way too, and there's a lot of overlap in the reasons why.

Women feel invisible when they are:

⇨ Not heard
⇨ Not acknowledged - whether it's a simple "hey, how are you" or referring to their achievements or accomplishments

⇨ Undervalued
⇨ Underpaid
⇨ Not appreciated

And finally:

When they are unsure of their own identity and how it has changed

That last point is a big one. It probably hit you right in the solar plexus (that's your gut, for those who are not chakra savvy). If you don't know who you are, then neither do the other people in your life. When you're disconnected from yourself, it's hard to communicate about who you are.

What I do is help clients showcase who they are through what they're wearing - their style. Your style gives you the power to decide what part of your personality you are allowing the world to see. You have the *power and control* to walk into a room, and show off any part of yourself in the best ways. Sometimes, you just need the guidance to get to that point.

Let's do a quick exercise. This is something that I do with ALL of my new clients. Describe yourself in 3 words. You, yourself as the individual - not your style, just you. Allow yourself to write down the first three words that come to mind, and don't overthink it. Write down or say the first three words to describe who you are, and there are no wrong answers.

Now take a look at what you wrote. How does that feel? Do you see that in how you dress? Are you allowing people to see who you really are?

Here we go.

I am officially giving you the power and permission to stop following rules (let's be clear, I'm talking about fashion rules here, not like basic societal rules. You still have to pay your taxes, credit card bills, follow traffic lights, and all that stuff). Growing up, I am sure that you heard all kinds of rules about style and fashion. You probably learned these rules from other individuals in your life, or magazines you read as a teenager, the internet, whatever, and all of that content made you think that you don't have any other choices when it comes to style. So, I am here, to step in and tell you that you are allowed to make the decisions that are best for YOU as an unique and powerful individual. I do this for men too, but it's more important for women, because we're always struggling with being seen and being heard.

I am giving you the power to allow you to show up as yourself. Not what other people expect you to be. Not what you think people want to see. Just you: those three words you wrote down describing yourself. As much (or as little) of you as you want to show. You can choose to show off one of those words or all of them. It's completely up to you, and how you're feeling that day. Your outfit doesn't need to tell your entire life story, and neither do you.

> You have the power and the control to show off as much of yourself as you feel comfortable doing.

Some days, I choose outfits that say, "THIS IS ME! HERE I AM! I am ready for you!" and other days, it's more "Hey guys, I'm Susan. Nice to meet you, I'll be over here sipping my coffee, enjoy your day." I'm always representing myself, as I want to be seen. Some days my message through my outfit is louder than others. It's your decision how loud you want your message to be. All that I ask is that you choose a message to communicate.

Your message can be, "I'm bold, and love meeting new people." and can be highlighted by strong, bright colors. Another message can be, "I love to travel, and am dying for a way to talk about it," so try wearing prints that have connections to some of your favorite destinations. Your message can even be, "New situations scare me, I'm intimidated by meeting new people, but I am friendly, once we start chatting," in which case, feel free to wear muted colors with an occasional pop of jewel tone, and maybe throw in a delicate, but unique piece of jewelry. It will take the right kind of person (your kind of person), to notice the detail in your jewelry, and spark a safe conversation.

> All I'm asking is that you don't hide behind your clothes.

You're hiding behind your clothes:

- ⇨ If they don't reflect anything about you
- ⇨ You hate your clothes, but you wear them anyway
- ⇨ You didn't choose your clothes

I want you to have strong, positive, emotional reactions to your clothes. The clothes in your closet, and the clothes you put on your body, should feel good, and you should feel great about yourself.

Every.

Time.

You.

Get.

Dressed.

It shouldn't matter where you're going or how you are currently feeling about your body, and what else is going on in your life. You should always feel great about yourself, and how you're showing up.

We can be afraid to change our wardrobe for a lot of different reasons. One of the biggest reasons we're afraid is because it forces us to see our body for how they are right now, in this exact moment. This is difficult no matter how your body has changed. Even if your body hasn't changed over the years, YOU as a person have. You've grown, evolved, and if you're reading this book now, you either really like me - in which case, "thanks, babe" - or you are at a time in your life where you are ready to step into a more empowered version of yourself.

As a stylist, something that I hear a lot is "I love that, but I can't wear that" or "that wouldn't look good on me." While it is definitely important to understand your individual body and how to dress it to accentuate its amazing shape, there aren't any rules about clothing being "out of your league."

It's easy to get stuck in a clothing rut, where we end up only wearing certain styles or colors. We start to believe that we only look good in those things because we think that they hide the parts of our bodies that we don't like. Those of you who only dress in black or dark colors, I'm definitely talking to you!

However, the rest of you are not excluded from this either. Getting dressed and buying clothes should not be about hiding parts of you that you don't like. It should be about accentuating what you love about yourself.

If you are used to hiding with your clothes, or allowing other people to shine, I can understand that looking at bright colors and prints can be intimidating. Something that I do with all of my clients is I always start by showing them pieces that I like that are within their comfort zone, and then I slowly branch out of their comfort zone to show them options that they may not have considered before working with me. A client once told me that he had never owned a cardigan, before I purchased one for him. I was shocked! After working together, I showed him how he could wear his new cardigan with several different pieces in his wardrobe, and he has really opened up to the idea of cardigans. That may sound silly to some of you, but just like that client, it's so important to be open-minded with clothes! Oftentimes, restricting yourself with what you can/can't wear is connected to limiting beliefs. When you're stuck in this mindset, the fear of judgement (being judged) plays a big part. So, instead of trying new things or experimenting with our clothes, we play it safe.

After having that interaction with my client, I tried my best to think about a single article of clothing that I have never had in my closet. The only thing that I could think of was parachute pants (think: MC Hammer). I think it's because I was born a little too late. I personally have always been willing to try new styles.

> Being adventurous with your style doesn't just come as a result of wanting to be on trend.

Think about trying new styles like you try new foods. If you tried pizza for the first time at a school cafeteria, you might say that you hate pizza, and you never want to eat it again. Pizza just isn't the food for you. But, if you go to Manco & Manco's in Ocean City, and try pizza for the first time there, you might decide that pizza is the only food that you want to eat for the rest of your life. Style is the same way. If you try a certain look or a specific color, and you have a negative experience with it, you may think, "oh ugh, no. No way am I wearing that ever again. I just can't wear _____." But, if you have a positive experience, you can learn about how the right shade of purple really makes your eyes pop, and that makes you feel like you are shining.

By trying new styles (and food), you're learning more about yourself through the process. The right clothes can have a transformative property on a person's mood. Once you learn that, you understand how you can feel incredible about yourself every day, no matter what else is going on in your life.

I do this for myself often! While working on this book, one example came to mind, and I share it especially for the moms who are reading this. When I was in the early stages of launching my business, and I first launched my blog, I did a photo shoot for a blog post about mixing patterns. I was just getting over being sick. I caught the Hand, Foot, and Mouth virus from my son's daycare. Both he and my husband already had it, and it skipped me the first time it plagued our house. Once the daycare got another round of Hand, Foot, and Mouth, it was my turn. Ugh, it's the worst! As much as I absolutely love patterns, I was definitely not a fan of the red dots all over my hands and feet...and arms and legs. But, after they started to heal a little bit, I put on some fun clothes that make me feel completely empowered, did the photo shoot, and completely forgot about my spots!

When you change your wardrobe at a point in your life when you are in transition, it's scary. It's the final piece to allow you to fully dive into that next phase. By holding on to your old clothes, you allow yourself to hold on to the past. You keep yourself in the place you were before you started making these changes in your life. So, by making the changes in your closet, it forces you to look deep into yourself, and ask: "Do these clothes really represent who I am, and who I want to be?"

Go back to your three words. Who are you? How do YOU describe yourself?

Dressing who you are now is part of it, so slowly incorporate dressing as who you want to be. I'm sure that you're familiar with the phrase, "Dress for the job you want." It's such a common phrase because by dressing for your dream job, you're starting the conversation about how qualified you are before you even actually start talking. People see you, and they make a positive assumption about you. You can have that same ability in your everyday life.

What I want to make clear is that you have choices in your personal style.

Rules are available to give you guidance, but you should always feel authentic, and feel seen like yourself.

As a stylist, I help you figure out what it means to you, as an unique individual, to show up as your authentic self, and I connect it to your personal style. I take those three words that you wrote down to describe yourself, and I help guide you through choosing pieces to reflect those aspects of your identity (while also factoring in your lifestyle, budget, and all of that good stuff that makes up your real life).

When you feel authentic, everything feels aligned. You're showing up as the best version of yourself, and people respond well to that! Take the time to think about how you would want other people to describe you, when you're not in the room, and start connecting with that. Make sure that the way that you dress also reflects those characteristics. If there's a disconnect, you need to examine what's going on, and why that's happening.

How do we determine our personality and our style?

Know yourself first and foremost. If you can't describe yourself, you can't create an aligned style. Go to my website and get my freebie that has a series of questions and guided meditation to look inward and discover yourself. It will also help you to visualize your style!

THE REASONS YOU'RE NOT WEARING THE CLOTHES IN YOUR CLOSET: FIT, PERSONALITY, AND EMOTIONS

Intuition Intuition Intuition Intuition Intuition Intuition

When the seasons change, do you find that you don't have anything in your closet that you actually want to wear? You've started to mentally prepare for the next season, and you're ready for the temperature change, but your wardrobe doesn't really reflect that. So, what can you do to make sure that you're actually wearing the clothes hanging in your closet?

Take a quick look at the pieces in your closet. Are there items in there that haven't been worn in over a year? (meaning, you didn't wear them the last time this upcoming season had arrived) There's always a good reason why we're not wearing something that's in our closet. It's usually a result of at least one of three different reasons: *fit, style, and emotions.*

● Fit ●

What is it that makes us hold on to these clothes? They don't fit. You're not wearing them. Why are they still taking up space in your closet?

Sometimes we're not wearing something in our closet, because the fit is just "off" – too big, too small, unbalanced proportions, awkward lengths, etc. When you're considering ideal fit, this can absolutely vary depending on how comfortable you feel in clothes. You may choose a size that fits looser or tighter around certain areas of your body because that's how you feel confident.

That being said, let's talk about "ideal fit" dealbreakers. Some "ideal fit" deal breakers include: the placement of the shoulder seam on a top, making sure the garment isn't falling off of your body in any way, nothing is too tight that it prevents proper circulation, and the length of the sleeves or hem don't affect your ability to function. In these fit situations, you can ask yourself, "is it worth getting it tailored?" to fix the problem with the fit. If it's not, you don't need it in your life.

How do you know if something is worth getting tailored? Ask yourself how much work needs to be done to make it something that you'll want to wear. Do your pants, skirt, or dress just need to be hemmed? Maybe a button on your jacket needs to move a little bit? Does that dress need to be taken in?

> Weigh your investment with how much use you will gain from the alterations.

If it's something basic like moving a button or hemming a pair of pants, that's easy! It's also inexpensive! You can even get your pants hemmed at a local dry cleaner, if you don't have a go-to tailor. When the alterations that need to occur include shortening sleeves, taking in a jacket, or adjusting the shoulders, be prepared for a bigger financial investment in the garment.

You will also want to seek out a tailor for more involved alterations. Sometimes these investments are completely worth it! If it means that you will have a perfectly tailored piece in your closet that will become a staple in your life, then get those alterations and make that investment! If the alterations cost more than it would to buy a replacement garment (of similar quality), then maybe you're better off looking for a replacement. This can be tricky when it comes to vintage pieces, because sometimes they're so unique and one of a kind, that you won't be able to find a replacement easily. So, think about how much you will actually end up wearing the piece, if it is perfectly altered.

● Not Your Style ●

We evolve so much with age and experience, and it's easy to say how we are no longer the person we once were. I mean, stop and think about where you were 5 years ago. What did a normal week look like for you then? What kinds of things did you enjoy doing in your free time? Do you still live in the same place? Are you still in the same job, with the same job title and responsibilities? Has your body changed in the last 5 years? What relationships have come and gone, or just evolved over that time?

How much in your life has changed in that amount of time? More importantly, how much of YOU has changed? But for some reason, your sense of style isn't always included in that life change upgrade. You expect yourself to continue to wear clothes that reflect a previous version of yourself that is no longer an accurate depiction of who you are. You don't have to remove every piece of clothing that you had from that time in your life, just remove the pieces that no longer reflect who you are now.

Sometimes, my clients struggle with knowing who they are, especially after going through major life changes. They need to work through emotional or energetic blocks. This "therapy" can sometimes be done through talking during one of our sessions, but in some cases, my clients need a different kind of guidance.

Guided meditations are one of my favorite modalities to help my clients view themselves in the way that they truly want to be seen. Through guided meditation, I help my clients to reconnect with their bodies and welcome in their higher self. The responses my clients give to the questions I ask during their meditation are from a deeper place. They respond naturally, rather than overthinking their answers. Their responses are guided by their intuition, and it's exactly how they feel in that specific moment in time. It's a beautiful way to begin our journey together. If you're interested in trying this meditation for yourself, it's available on my website susanpadronstylist.com.

● Your style should match your personality ●

It can be in big, obvious ways, or in a subtle way, but you should always show up as you. If you're not wearing something due to style conflicts, it's because your subconscious is saying, "this isn't you" or "you've changed."

One of my dear friends and clients, Ilia, shared her feelings about how her style had to evolve in order to regain her sense of self. In less than ten years, she became a mom to twin boys, and left her career as a social worker to start her own business as an energy worker. When Ilia and I went through her closet together, it was filled with hand-me-downs from well intentioned friends and family. While hand-me-downs can be a perfect fit, it can also be a problem when they take up the majority of your closet. Why? Because hand-me-downs don't allow you to make a choice. Hand-me-downs aren't a conscious decision that you're making to say, "This is what I want to own. This is what I want to wear, because this feels like me."

The evolution into motherhood, leaving a career, starting a new business, and rediscovering yourself as soon as the winds of change calm down from hurricane level to a calm breeze - I always enjoyed my clothes when I was a teacher, but it was hard embracing a new identity as a stylist, while wearing the same clothes I wore in the classroom. I felt like if I still looked like a teacher, I wouldn't be perceived as a stylist. The worst was when I had to meet with a client after teaching all day. Wearing those same clothes made me feel like an imposter. It was almost like my clients could smell the chalk and middle school student awkwardness. I felt like I needed to prove myself. I'm sure my energy came across as insecure, and the vibe I gave off was, "I really AM a personal stylist! I promise!!" That kind of desperate, insecure energy is not a good look.

Once I had left teaching to pursue styling full time, it took some soul searching to figure out what I wanted my identity to look like as a stylist. I had a brand new identity with all of this freedom. I'm a Scorpio (sun) with a Sagitarius moon rising, so I need freedom. You put me in a box, and I freak out, not because I'm claustrophobic, but because the box makes me feel too limited.

But, when you have the ability to show up completely as yourself, with only yourself to hold you back, it's a daunting process. While you have this unlimited freedom, it can be hard to just take a step back, and ask yourself, "Who am I?"

I remember standing in my closet looking at my beautiful clothes. I edit my own closet about once a year, but once I left teaching, my closet and I got real intimate. I went through EVERYTHING. Every single piece in my closet, and I purged so many things. I got rid of boring trousers, business casual sweaters, and SO MANY pieces that I held on to for "when I got back to my pre baby weight/body."

Here's the thing: having a baby changed my body. It also changed my life. Allow me to briefly inform you of the four surgeries I had in four years after Honey Bunny was born, along with an endometriosis diagnosis, and my body is completely different than it was before I had a baby. And that's all okay. It didn't feel okay right away, and we'll talk about that later. I share all of that with you because if you have a similar story, I want you to know that you're not alone. If you don't have a similar story, and your body looks almost identical to how it did before you had your baby, or it looks the same as you did in college, there's of course nothing wrong with that, either. The point I'm trying to make crystal clear is that no matter what your body looks like, when you go through life, you change, and your style changes as a result.

After I finished my major closet purge, I saw me in my clothes and in my closet. I was able to shed who I used to be in order to allow my new self to start showing up fully.

● Emotions/Sentimental Reasons ●

Emotions are tricky. The way that they creep into our clothes can be through memories associated with an outfit, and people or words associated with the clothing item. When there are negative emotions, or bad energy connected to clothes, they attach, and don't leave. You always have that emotion tied to the clothing item, and it will prevent you from wanting to wear it.

Even if you are not thinking about that specific memory, the negative energy from that event is still present. You're subconsciously detecting the energy, being repelled by it, and you don't want to wear those clothes.

Here's what I'm talking about:

⇨   "I wore this to my _____'s funeral."

⇨   "This is what I was wearing when I met my ex."

⇨   "My mom said this reminds her of a couch she used to have."

⇨   "My son hates this dress."

Emotions around clothes can also become complicated when the clothes are viewed as sentimental. Holding on to clothes for sentimental reasons is probably the trickiest out of all of these reasons that you're not wearing the clothes in your closet.

Let's start by talking about what doesn't count as sentimental. If you're looking at a piece of clothing in your closet, and you already know that it doesn't fit, and you don't love it, you might be tempted to hold on to it because it feels sentimental. It's common to feel this way if you received the garment as a gift, especially if your relationship with the gift giver is somewhat complicated.

Removing that piece of clothing from your closet is not going to cause a war between the two of you. If the piece of clothing being absent from your closet does cause any conflict, just say that your friend, Susan, needed to borrow it. ;)

Another time that something is not considered sentimental is when you get the clothing item for free at an event. "But it was free! I feel bad getting rid of it" or "It's a perfectly good t-shirt/sweatshirt/etc!" Something to consider when you're wearing free stuff: typically, when you get something for free, especially at an event, the item has a company's name and/or logo on it. How much do you know about that company? Do you feel strongly enough in support of them that you want to walk around doing free advertising for them? Do you like the company so much that you want people to associate it with you?

It's complicated because you can easily attach a memory to an outfit.

◐ Because that memory holds sentimental ◑ value to you, the outfit does too

So, how do you end up with a wardrobe filled with only clothes that you love? Go through your closet one section at a time, if you don't have the time to tackle it all at once. Another way is to make a day of it – put it on your schedule and Get. It. Done.

This last option is more of an ongoing approach. When you are getting dressed, and put something on, if you take it off right away, because you don't like the way it looks, don't just hang it back in your closet. Set it aside, so that when you have the time, you can add it to your, "it doesn't have to go home, but it can't stay here" collection.

What are your thoughts on sustainable fashion?

There are different ways to avoid fast fashion - buying from sustainable brands, shopping secondhand/thrifting, or renting clothes. Sometimes brands that are sustainable can appear to be at a higher price point, but in addition to the positive impact these brands are having on the planet, the quality of the pieces is also typically higher.

HAND-ME-DOWNS: NOT JUST FOR CLOTHES

In Marie Forleo's book, *Everything is Figureoutable*, there were so many nuggets of wisdom, but there was a specific topic that really jumped out at me: hand-me-down beliefs.[1]

In the chapter, "The Magic of Belief," Marie Forelo discusses the concept of "hand-me-down beliefs." Hand-me-down beliefs are ideas that are passed down, with the best of intentions. They can influence many different areas of your life, and you believe them, because they're usually told to you by your loved ones. But, then you grow, change, and evolve, and you start to feel some dissonance surrounding those beliefs. You might realize that they're, in fact, not yours, and they actually don't apply to you. As soon as I heard about "hand-me-down beliefs," I immediately felt a connection to style rules.

Let's list some style rules that I'm sure you've heard before:

1. You can't wear white after Labor Day
2. You can only wear horizontal stripes if you're tall and thin.
3. You should dress yourself strictly based on your body type.
4. Women over the age of _____ can't wear _____.
5. Nylons/tights must be worn to look professional.

[1]Forleo, Marie. *Everything is Figureoutable*. New York: Portfolio, Penguin Books. 2019. https://www.marieforleo.com/

6.   You can't mix black and blue or black and brown.

7.   Your shoes have to match your belt, or your purse has to match your shoes.

You probably heard even more rules that were specific to your body, culture, or family. While these "rules" can absolutely help give you a starting point to create your own style, it's normal to reach a point where they no longer apply.

Think about it. Your life changes, your body changes, and your career may change too. You can't expect those rules to apply consistently, when your life doesn't remain consistent.

Consider any other kind of hand-me-down, whether it's a thought process, type of clothing, or piece of furniture – at some point, you may want to replace it with something you chose on your own.

I hear grown women tell me, "I can't wear that, because they said (insert preconceived notions here)"

● When Rules Help ●

As a personal stylist, do I give my clients rules to follow while we're shopping? Yes. They're not terribly strict rules, but I do provide guidance for them, so that they can have efficiency in their morning routine. The rules are also specific to them as an individual, which is exactly how you should take on style advice (or any advice in life). Take what applies to you and what feels good, and let the rest pass you by.

As soon as you start focusing on how you feel in an outfit, and you care less about what hypothetical judgements you will receive, the more confident you will be able to enter situations in your life.

Q&A

How do you deal with "imposter syndrome?" What's your advice for your clients?

Begin with pieces that are still within your comfort zone, so you can avoid "can I really wear something like this?" Starting with one part of your outfit that is a little outside your comfort zone, and give yourself time to become comfortable with it. You'll naturally branch out more and more as you experiment! It won't feel as jarring if you go slowly.

LOVE YOUR CLOSET:
DREAMS DO
COME TRUE

What does it look like to have a closet filled with pieces that you love? It will look different for everyone! It depends on what pieces speak to you, right?

The way that I like to explain it, so that it applies to everyone is you should have a wardrobe with your "workhorse" pieces, "statement" pieces, and "chameleon" pieces.

● Workhorse pieces ●

These are also occasionally called "basics" or "staples," meaning that they are worn often, because they are versatile, and somewhat neutral. For me, my workhorse pieces are good pairs of high-waisted jeans, a unique blazer, and a good v-neck, white t-shirt. I invest in my jeans, because I know I'm going to wear them a lot, and I will not be delicate with them (Honey Bunny won't be either, because small child things).

A unique blazer is something that I'll grab before I leave the house, and it instantly elevates an outfit. I could be taking care of things around the house, wearing a graphic t-shirt and jeans, like I often do, and all I need to do to elevate the outfit is add my unique blazer, some cool accessories (jewelry and a hat), and a pair of heeled booties, and I look like I put a lot of effort into an outfit that's actually easy and comfortable.

Workhorse pieces get bonus points if they rarely wrinkle because it makes them even easier to just grab them and go.

◉ Statement pieces ◉

Statement pieces can be accessories, shoes, outerwear, or clothes. They are usually bold in the way that they stand out from an outfit. They can be a bright color, pattern, sparkly, shiny, textured, or all of the above. It really depends on how you relate to making a statement with your outfit. From the years I've spent working with clients as a personal stylist, I have learned that everyone has a different definition of their statement pieces.

My favorite statement pieces are also versatile, so that I can wear them in different ways without it being too memorable. A big concern that I often hear is, "I don't want people to think that I wear this all the time." When your statement piece is versatile, people remember that your outfit looked bold, and they don't just associate you with that individual piece.

One of my statement pieces that I wear on repeat in the fall is a pair of studded booties. I wear them with jeans, dresses, joggers... basically everything. I never hear, "You wear those booties all the time," because my outfit is always different, and I also radiate the energy of "yeah, I wear these booties all the time, because they're one of the coolest things I own, and they work with everything. Wouldn't you wear them all the time if they resonated with you?"

◉ Chameleon pieces ◉

A chameleon piece is something that can be worn in many different ways, and it can also work for casual or dressy situations with some easy modifications. Like a chameleon, these pieces just need subtle changes to work with their surroundings. A moto jacket is a favorite chameleon piece because it can be worn over a dress or with a t-shirt and distressed jeans. Black pointed toe pumps are another fantastic chameleon piece. They can be worn with a pencil skirt and button down shirt, for a classic, work appropriate outfit.

You can wear them with faux leather leggings, and a bodysuit to go out with your friends. Black pointed toe pumps can also be worn with a pair of wide leg, high waisted jeans, and a vintage t-shirt, and a black panama hat for a boho rockstar chic look. The options are practically endless with the versatility of those kinds of shoes, hence why they make such great chameleon pieces in your closet.

The next time you go shopping, look at what you want to buy, and ask yourself what category it falls into: workhorse, statement, or chameleon. It helps to have a balance of all three, with the most emphasis on your workhorse and chameleon pieces.

If you find that you have a lot of statement pieces in your closet, challenge yourself to see if any of them can work in the other two categories. If not, it's time to add some more versatile clothes to your collection.

● Confidence ●

Are you guilty of buying something because it "looked good on someone else?" Maybe you have a stylish friend, and you love everything she wears. So, you ask her to buy you things when she goes shopping. The pieces she selects for you fit your body perfectly, but for some strange reason, they just feel wrong when you're wearing them.

Even if the person you used as style inspiration has the exact same body type and coloring as you, it doesn't mean that their style matches yours. It's possible that you picked up on their confidence that they were exuding, and wanted to match that rather than match outfits. You might not truly want to dress like your friend, but what you really want is to walk through life with total self confidence like she does.

When your friend gets dressed, she puts her clothes on, accessorizes herself, does a final outfit check in the mirror, and then goes about her day without a second thought about it. Her final outfit check confirmed she felt and looked good, so as long as she doesn't have any major wardrobe malfunctions throughout her day, she'll continue to look great.

Let's talk about what it looks like when someone is wearing confidence. It shows in how they carry themselves. When someone is wearing confidence, they walk into a room with ease, and they make it all look effortless. It appears that way because they're most likely not thinking about what they're wearing, how people are viewing them, or how they appear to others.

Believe it or not, confidence and comfort go hand in hand. If you're uncomfortable in what you're wearing, it will show in how you carry yourself. Whether you're uncomfortable, because your outfit doesn't fit your body or your personal style, your energy will reflect it. You will look insecure, because in that outfit, you are insecure. You don't feel like you are representing yourself as your best self. You are uncomfortable with how your body appears, and you feel that people are thinking about you in ways that conflict with your view of yourself.

If you feel like you are constantly unsure of what to wear, take a few deep, cleansing breaths, before you get dressed in the morning. Connect with yourself and your body in a brief moment of calm and quiet, and see what intuitively feels good to wear in that moment.

As a stylist, what does "your style should match your personality" really mean for your clients?

Your clothes, shoes, and accessories should feel like an extension of you. By matching your style to your personality, you're allowing your style to speak for you. Think about all of the times you have seen someone, and felt a connection to them, because you liked what they were wearing. Maybe you even approach that person and compliment what they're wearing. By saying "I really like your _____", you're creating an opportunity for connection between yourself and another person.

SHADOW SIDE

BODY ACCEPTANCE: ACCEPTANCE HAPPENS AFTER FORGIVENESS

This is not a chapter about how I lost the baby weight and loved my body again. This is not a chapter about how I gained weight and loved my body again. This section is about how I got to a place in my life where I love my body, because of everything we've been through together.

When Honey Bunny was 5 months old, I had my first of four surgeries in four years. Two of those surgeries were on my left knee, and bookended my running hobby. The other two surgeries were for endometriosis.

My body changed so much during that time, and I was just beginning to get reintroduced to my body since having a baby. I spent a lot of my post surgery recovery time feeling betrayed by my body. I was angry, frustrated, and hurt that my body wasn't healthy or okay. I had lots of reasons (excuses) why I gained weight, and I felt like I needed to explain those reasons whenever someone new in my life saw a picture of "how I used to look."

It wasn't that my body betrayed me; it was that I let my body down. I wasn't listening to her. I didn't give her what she needed. All I could focus on was "why don't you feel better?" "Why aren't you better yet?" She was sad, and I wasn't paying attention.

So often I hear, "When I lose the weight, I'll buy myself new clothes." That's fair, but only when coming from the mentality of "when my body changes, and my clothes no longer fit, I need to buy new clothes (or get them altered)." That's where I find the problem, because the majority of the time, the emphasis isn't on the body changing, but it's on the body becoming smaller, taking up less space. So, I'm here to tell you all to stop being hypocrites. Open your mind to all of the ways your body can change, and allow yourself to find clothes that feel good no matter the changes.

Whenever I am inevitably asked the question, "who has been your most challenging client?" my response has been the same, for several years now. The answer: clients with body dysmorphia. Body dysmorphia can essentially be described as a mental health condition where a person can only focus on a perceived flaw on their body. This flaw is either minor or imagined by the person with body dysmorphia, and therefore, unless that person seeks treatment, there is nothing that anyone can do to help them see themselves otherwise.

It's heartbreaking because there is truly nothing that I can say or do to help someone with body dysmorphia to fully love themselves. If they're not ready, honestly, we shouldn't be working together.

I'm not saying that you have to love everything about yourself (although that is the dream, right?), but try not to obsess over the little things, perceived big things, or any of the things that you hate about your body.

ENDOMETRIOSIS: THE DIAGNOSIS THAT RATTLED ME

Shadow Side Shadow Side Shadow Side Shadow Side

Quick disclaimer: I am not a doctor or any kind of medical professional. I am only sharing my experiences with endometriosis, as a way to help spread awareness and encourage discussion. If you have any questions about your individual health, or think you may have endometriosis, please contact your doctor immediately.

It was a Tuesday, the day after I had a huge shoot in NY in April 2018. I picked up Honey Bunny from my parents' house, hit some traffic on the way home, and got Bunny a snack. Just went about the day as normal, because at the time, it was.

I used the bathroom, and after, I started to experience pain. The pain quickly escalated from "this is uncomfortable" to not being able to think straight. I curled up on the floor, because anything else was pretty unbearable. Suddenly I was drenched in sweat, and any kind of pressure on my abdomen was torture. There was a sharp, stabbing pain primarily on the right side of my lower abdomen, but the pain ran across to the left as well.

Thankfully, Tony came home from work right around that point, and I told him, "I'm not okay, I need to go to the hospital."

So, the three of us go to the ER. Tony called his sister to meet us at the hospital to take Honey Bunny back to our house, since we had no idea how long we would be there. Honey Bunny was great while he was there with us. He was so well behaved and understanding, I was very proud of him. While we were still in the waiting room, my sister-in-law arrived and took Bunny to our house.

Not too long after that, they took me to a room. A doctor came in to ask me about my symptoms, and examined my abdomen. His immediate thoughts were either a cyst or my appendix, so the next step were diagnostic tests.

More waiting and tests later, the doctor comes back: "Well, I found some things. You have a complex cyst called an endometrioma on your left ovary. It looks like it ruptured, so you have fluid and blood in your abdomen, which is causing the discomfort. Follow up with your OBGYN, and you should feel better in a few days." He provided a little more information than that, but that's the majority of what he said. He answered a few questions I had, which was helpful, and started the discharge process.

Another doctor came into my room and made sure that I had an OBGYN that I see. She suggested that I talk to my OBGYN about getting an MRI. This doctor was surprisingly insistent on it. I didn't ask her why she felt this way. I was still in a lot of pain, and I was eager to go home.

The doctor left, and a nurse came in with my discharge paperwork. She casually said, "Here's some information on endometriosis for you to look over." And she immediately left the room.

I felt my heart drop.

She just handed me the stack of papers, and left the room. Tony was with me the whole time. At some point after that, I think as we were walking out to the car, I said to him, "So, I have endometriosis."

◗

I made an appointment with a doctor at my OBGYN practice for the next day. She reassured me that I would feel better in a few days, but if not, we talked about the treatment option she recommended. I have a genetic mutation called Factor II Prothrombin, which puts me at a predisposition for getting blood clots. That means, taking birth control, which is commonly used as a way to manage endometriosis, is not an option for me.

The treatment she suggested was Lupron[1], an injection that puts your body into medically induced menopause. It didn't sound great, but we agreed that we would see how I felt, and discuss it in more detail if it came to that.

After leaving that appointment, I began to do my own research on Lupron and was pretty horrified. The side effects were awful, with a lot of them being long term, and they do quite a bit of damage to the body along the way. But, I wasn't sure if I had any other options, and she said I should feel better in a few days, so maybe all of this would just go away.

By then, it had been six days.

Six is more than a few.

I knew this was not normal or okay, so I did something about it. I called my doctor's office again. I made an appointment for the doctor that had the first available appointment at my OBGYN practice, and it happened to be a different doctor than I had seen the first time.

He reviewed the first doctor's suggestions, and strongly disagreed. Then he told me that he rarely suggests Lupron as a form of treatment to his patients, especially to someone as young as I am (I'm pretty sure I did a "no, stop, thank you" hair toss every time he said "for someone as young as you"). If I were closer to menopausal age, it would be a different story. He said (and this is an exact quote), "It would wreak havoc on your body." And he reiterated that it would not do anything for my pain or discomfort, even if we started

[1] For more information on Lupron, please visit http://www.lupron.com/

it today (which is not even an option, because insurance companies make you jump through hoops to get it). He was suggesting surgery.

Something to keep in mind, when it comes to endometriosis, at the time while this book is being written, there is no cure. There is a lot of controversial data that suggests doing a total hysterectomy with bilateral salpingo-oophorectomy (removing the uterus, cervix, fallopian tubes, and ovaries) can cure endometriosis. It's controversial because if the endometrial tissue has implanted on other organs, and not all of it is removed during the surgery, you will not be cured. That being said, there is no cure. However, laparoscopic surgery is the one way to remove the endometrial tissue and the endometrioma (complex cyst) that had set up camp in my body.

We both agreed that surgery was my best option, and the doctor told me that the surgical scheduler would call me to set up the surgery.

The rest of the day passed by, and no phone call. The next morning passed, and still no phone call. So, I called them. Apparently, my doctor still had not sent over the referral for my surgery (I'm sorry, what?!), but the surgical scheduler checked to see when his next available surgery date is.

June fucking 8th.

For those of you keeping track of timing, my trip to the ER was in April, which means that I would have had to live couch bound, in pain, not able to fully function in any aspect of my life, for about a month and a half. I hung up the phone with the surgical scheduler and cried. I cried a lot. Like, A LOT a lot.

I calmed down, eventually, and once I calmed down, I called them back.

Not only did I call them, but I called them back multiple times a day, leaving a message for both doctors I saw, asking to speak with a nurse, or the surgical scheduler in any attempt to change the date of my surgery to sooner. I am convinced that I annoyed almost everyone in my doctor's office, which I am completely fine with, and you better believe that never stopped me from continuing to try. Someone from the office called me back saying "now, who is it that you want to talk to?" To say that she sounded irritated with me is an understatement.

But ya know what? She wasn't even close to as frustrated and irritated as I was about the fact that I was told to wait a month and a half, before I could have any relief from debilitating pain.

Why am I telling you about how I harassed my doctor's office with phone calls? Because even when you feel like you're at your weakest, you're strong. The strength you need to fight for yourself, and be your own advocate is always there. Sometimes there is another option; you just have to find it.

Finally, on Friday, I received a (helpful) call back.

> My surgery was scheduled, and it was weeks earlier than the original date they gave me. Instead of waiting weeks, I only had to wait days, and I could finally breathe.

I checked in at the waiting room, and before long they took me back to the room. I met with the nurse, my doctor, the anesthesiologist (spelled that on the first try!), and a couple of medical students that were going to be observing my surgery. Tony commented on how many people were going to be watching my surgery, to which I replied, "I hope it's entertaining for them."

Tony quickly responded, "I don't! I hope it's boring!" and I immediately saw his point.

With every meeting of medical personnel, they asked me the same questions: my name, birthdate, a series of medical history questions, and what I was having done during surgery. The doctor answered all of my questions and Tony's, and he was very patient with us. He explained that the surgery could take anywhere between 1 and 2 hours depending on what he found during the surgery. Depending on the condition of my left ovary (the one with the cyst), the possibility of needing to remove the ovary and fallopian tube was something he wanted to mention, but he thought was highly unlikely.

After all of the introductions and confirmation of information was completed, I met the nurse anesthetist (did not spell that on the first..or second try). She told me that she just gave me a sedative, "if that's okay."

"Um, of course, it is!" I responded, and they started wheeling my bed out of the room to the OR. I vaguely remember entering the OR, and that's it. I woke up in recovery.

It took about an hour before I could keep my eyes open.

Tony came in to help me get dressed, and he filled me in on what my doctor shared with him while I was in recovery. My doctor said that everything went well! He drained and removed the cyst that was on my left ovary, and he was able to remove all of the signs of endometriosis in my abdomen. All of this was done with just three little incisions. One on either side near my hips, and one in my belly button.

My doctor called to check in at around lunch time the following day. We discussed the details of my surgery. He drained and removed the endometrioma on my left ovary. The doctor also removed all of the endometrial implants that were in front and behind my uterus. Thankfully, everything looked fine! I remember feeling relieved, but at the same time, I knew it wasn't the end. Intuitively, I think I knew we would be doing this again sooner rather than later.

Writing about my experience with endometriosis was when I decided to dig deeper within myself. For the people with endometriosis who are reading this, I am going to ask you to do the same. I remember getting my period in 5th grade, before most of my friends. The cramps were pretty unbearable for a day or so every month. I would often black out from the pain, and throw up, but my mom and sister were like that, so I thought it was normal.

> Fun fact: "The cause of endometriosis is not yet known, but research does show that first-degree relatives of women with this disease have a seven-fold risk of developing endometriosis."
> – A direct quote from Endometriosis.org

As a teenager, talking about it with my doctor brought up conversations of going on oral contraceptives, but if you recall from earlier in our story, that's no longer an option for me. Even when I did mention at my annual appointment with my OBGYN that I had really bad cramps, there were never follow up tests done. I remember one doctor telling me that "a lot of women experienced painful cramps and vomiting" (end scene.)

Is it possible that I have had endometriomas or signs of endometriosis before?

Are you ready for this?

About 1 out of 3 women consult 3 to 4 physicians before receiving an endometriosis diagnosis.*

*based on a self-reported 1998 Endometriosos Association survey of 4334 respondents reporting a surgiacl diagnosis of endometriosis.[2]

It's not just physicians that sometimes trivialize symptoms of endometriosis. I have a distinct memory of being in 7th grade social studies, where I was blacking in and out while sitting at my seat, feeling like I was going to throw up or pass out, suffering from horrible cramps. A good friend of mine sat across from me, and he noticed that I was not okay. He approached our teacher, and asked HER, if he could take me to the nurse.

Our teacher forced me to walk to her desk to explain what was wrong. When I described my symptoms to her, she rolled her eyes and dismissively said, "cramps don't hurt that much." Thankfully, she wrote me a pass to the nurse's office, but made me go alone.

My cramps continued with those types of symptoms, until I got pregnant with my son in 2014. Thankfully, I was able to get pregnant right away without any issues (30-40% of women with endometriosis experience infertility, making endometriosis one of the top 3 reasons for female infertility, according to Endofound.org). My cramps were SIGNIFICANTLY better after giving birth to Honey Bunny. It's also important to note that pregnancy can treat symptoms of endometriosis, but just like after surgery, it may come back.

Unfortunately, the reality for many patients is that

[2] Rebecca Greene, B.A., Pamela Stratton, M.D., Sean D. Cleary, Ph.D., Mary Lou Ballweg, B.A., and Ninet Sinaii, Ph.D. "Diagnostic experience among 4,334 women reporting surgically diagnosed endometriosis." *Fertility and Sterility* Vol. 91, No. 1, January 2009. Copyright 2009 American Society for Reproductive Medicine, Published by Elsevier Inc. doi:10.1016

endometriosis will come back; it's just a matter of when. Because female reproductive health is not something that is always comfortably discussed, it can be difficult to communicate why you can't function for a few days.

Speaking from my own experience, as a sole business owner, I found it very challenging to continue to work prior to my surgery. If I hadn't fought for my healthcare and treatment, it would have meant continuing to be limited to one "activity" a day, otherwise I would feel even worse the next day.

Budgeting my energy became crucial for any kind of productivity. That meant canceling a lot of plans and prioritizing work over social activities. It also meant understanding that if I felt exhausted by the afternoon, recharging by the night was not going to happen. Because of my symptoms and my genetic mutation, surgery was the best option for me.

> The biggest takeaways that I want you to have from all of this, whether you can personally relate it to endometriosis or not, are that you are not alone, you are stronger than you think, and you deserve to be heard.

After my endometriosis surgery in May 2018, I was pain free until June 5th 2018. I know, it's weird to know an exact date for when my pain came back. My doctor had recommended keeping a daily pain journal, following my surgery. This would help us figure out what step to take next. We both agreed that waiting three months after my surgery, while documenting my pain would be best, before we took any treatment actions. At the end of that three months, we would discuss if an IUD would be necessary to pause the endometriosis symptoms.

I didn't make it to that three months.

I started to have isolated, specific pain on my left side again, like I said, on June 5th. It would come and go, but it was intense, sharp, and very familiar. About a month after that, I had my annual gynecologist appointment, so I mentioned that the pain returned. My doctor told me to schedule an ultrasound, and left it up to me to continue to wait to the end of our three month mark, or move it up sooner. Initially, I was determined to wait it out. I only had about a month and a half left. That meant that I was halfway there.

I could do it, right? Nope.

I had three photo shoots in five days. Two of those shoots were in NYC and required a TON of heavy lifting. I felt horrible, but I powered through to prove something to myself (SO glad I don't do that anymore). For a long time, I felt like I needed to prove how "strong" I was. I thought asking or admitting that I needed help was a sign of weakness (it's not). It wasn't until I had been bleeding much more than usual, that I called my doctor. I moved up my ultrasound and appointment with him.

After the ultrasound was complete, I went to see my gynecologist. I was given the report from the ultrasound, before I left the imaging office. That was given to the doctor before I spoke with him. I explained to him how I had been feeling. He asked me how often I was pain free, to which I replied, "about five days a month."

It wasn't until I saw his face and heard his reply that it really sunk in for me: it's not normal to only be pain free for five days a month. My "normal" had become using my heat pack whenever I'm at home and taking multiple Advil when the pain completely interferes with my ability to function.

Then he told me that I had cysts on both ovaries. Good ol' lefty has a complex cyst again (what a bitch). Righty felt left out, I guess, so she had to have one too.

Next, he discussed my options. Birth control pills are the typical approach. I can't do that, because of Factor II Prothrombin gene mutation that makes me predisposed to blood clots (a super fun fact I often tell at parties. Just kidding, I don't go to parties.)

My option would be getting an IUD to suppress my periods. No period = no endometriosis, which is why pregnancy and menopause are great for endometriosis. However, because I was in pain, and the cysts were there, we needed to start with a "clean slate," which meant getting another surgery.

The plan was to schedule the surgery, and he'll implant the IUD once the surgery is completed. It would all be done at once, so I wouldn't need to have a separate appointment for the IUD implantation. He reassured me that he has had success with suppressing endometriosis symptoms with IUDs. The IUD that I will be getting can be replaced every five years. As long as the IUD keeps the endometriosis controlled, we can wait until I'm about 45, and then we'll remove my ovaries.

Tony and I feel very fulfilled having Honey Bunny in our lives. We have both agreed many times that we might just end up having Honey Bunny as our only child.

It's funny how your feelings about a decision can change when all of a sudden you no longer have a choice in the decision making. I'm not saying that the news I got makes me want to have another child immediately. What I am saying is that, I was surprised by how much I was mourning the future loss of my ovaries. I was concerned that I would be disappointing Tony and Honey Bunny, because now it would only be the three of us. I felt like my body betrayed me.

After we put Honey Bunny to bed, I was able to confide in Tony about how I was feeling. He listened, comforted, and validated me like no one else can. We talked through it all, and I no longer had the worries that I had prior to our conversation.

So, why am I getting all up close and personal with you about my feelings? Because just like in the other parts of this story, I want you to know that if you're going through this, you are not alone. Reach out. Speak up. Stop accepting constant pain as a way of life, because it's not.

At my follow up appointment in November, my doctor and I decided to go a slightly different route than we had initially discussed prior to my surgery. The original plan was to put in an IUD after completing the surgery. The universe decided that wasn't the right plan for me, and the IUD wasn't ready in time for my surgery. This led my doctor to pursuing other options. Enter the new drug, Orilissa[3].

My doctor consulted his colleagues about my specific situation – endometriosis presenting with an endometrioma on my ovary with

[3] For more information on Orilissa, please visit https://www.orilissa.com/

every occurrence, two surgeries in six months, genetic mutation that prevents me from taking birth control/hormones, not medically ready for a full hysterectomy with oophorectomy, blah blah blah. All of this made me the perfect candidate for a newish medication, Orilissa, specifically designed for endometriosis treatment.

It took me a month to get the medication. I was so excited to start taking my new meds and be on the road to recovery, that I took it on December 23rd. Again, why do I remember the specific date? Because, the next day, December 24th, was our annual Christmas Eve brunch that we host at our house. We have my in-laws over for brunch every year.

I took my first two doses of my new meds on the 23rd - 200mg twice a day. Felt totally fine.

Then, I woke up on Christmas Eve, and I couldn't lift my head without feeling dizzy and nauseous. I tried powering through, and even attempted to take a shower to try to feel better. After vomiting in said shower, I decided I couldn't host my own brunch. I ended up calling my doctor to figure out what to do. The doctor on call advised me to skip the doses for that day, give my body the day off tomorrow, and restart it again the day after Christmas. Eventually, at around 4pm, I felt somewhat human again.

While being sick on Christmas Eve wasn't fun, my biggest concern was, "this cannot be my new normal." Thankfully, when I took the medication again, I felt fine.

> Fun fact: when I mentioned my reaction to my doctor (6 weeks later), he told me it was normal. *(Thanks, Doc)*. A warning would have been nice, but it's possible that it might have made me apprehensive about starting the medication.

After taking Orilissa for almost 3 months, my pain levels decreased tremendously. I wasn't pain free, but a lot of my other symptoms from endometriosis had diminished or went away completely. I was having hot flashes as a side effect from the medication. They would happen about 5-7 times a day. It was pretty miserable, but it was way better than the intense pain I was feeling. I had to dress myself differently, and there were certain fabrics that I avoided completely.

The plan was that after three months, I would switch to the lower dose of 150mg once a day, and I would take that dose daily for two years. Once I hit the two year mark, I would stop it for a few months, and start the process again: 200mg 2x a day for 3 months followed by 150mg 1x a day for 2 years, a few months off, rinse and repeat until menopause, desired pregnancy, new and better medication comes out, etc.

After taking Orilissa for about five months, I started getting acupuncture. While my symptoms had diminished due to the medication, I was still in pain, and I was curious about what a pain free life could look like. To be honest, I was desperate for a pain free life, and I was willing to try almost anything. My mom had sent me an article about an acupuncture practice that specializes in female reproductive health. I booked my first appointment, and was hooked.

Every time I went in for an acupuncture treatment, I allowed myself to surrender. Sometimes I would try to meditate, but every time, I would be taken to a healing state of being. It was so relaxing. I loved it. I received acupuncture treatments for just shy of a year. I only stopped going because of the global pandemic, but thankfully, I was at a point in my treatment that it was more for maintenance than active treatment.

After taking Orilissa for 10 months, I was able to wean off of it with the support from my OBGYN and my acupuncturist. The more connected that I became with my body, the more resistance I had to taking the Orilissa. I can't really remember feeling that way before taking any medication. But for some reason, my body didn't like being in a constant state of hormonal limbo. I missed the natural stages of my cycle. My body didn't feel right. It took a few months after stopping the medication for my body to return to a normal cycle, but once it did, it felt freeing. I am really grateful for acupuncture, and its impact that it had on my endometriosis battle. Acupuncture really was the only thing that relieved my endometriosis pain.

The whole experience from being diagnosed with endometriosis to learning how to live with it felt like a lifetime of personal growth thrown into a couple of years. Suffering through pain silently, doesn't make you stronger.

Becoming my own health advocate allowed me to release the idea of myself as the "quiet one who stayed under the radar." I had let go of this version of myself in pieces over time, and my battle with endometriosis allowed me to let go of that final piece.

I have a voice, and it's meant to be heard.

ADDITIONAL RESOURCES

⇨ Hummelshoj, Lone, et al. Endometriosis.org, 2021, endometriosis.org/.

⇨ Inc., AbbVie. "Your Go-To Resource for Endometriosis." SPEAKENDO.COM, AbbVie Inc., 2020, speakendo.com/.

⇨ Petersen, Nancy. NancysNookEndo, 2021, nancysnookendo.com/.

⇨ The Endo Project, @theendoproject instagram.com/theendoproject

⇨ Emilia Victoria, @Livingwithendometriosis__ instagram.com/livingwithendometriosis__

⇨ Endometriosis Foundation of America, 2021. endofound.org/

CONFESSIONS OF A PERSONAL STYLIST: ARE YOU READY FOR THIS?

When you have a job that involves making other people look and feel good, there tends to be a lot of magic and curiosity surrounding not only what you do, but who you are.

Consider this a section of confessions about my personality, as well as little fun responses to questions I've received over the years.

● I wear ugly pajamas ●

I am not stylish all the time. Up until recently (and only out of necessity), my pajamas consisted of patterned (old) pajama pants and a concert t-shirt (either Dave Matthews Band or Mumford and Sons), or a t-shirt I acquired from a trip (one favorite is from a coffee shop in Stone Harbor that has "Decaf" in the universal "prohibited" or "no symbol"). These are paired with my slippers that I live in as soon as I enter my house.

This is exactly why, when I am going through my client's wardrobes, I specifically tell them that I do not need to go through what they wear to bed or to work out. Don't get me wrong, sometimes I do help clients with their pajamas and workout clothes, but it's usually when they struggle with knowing what they should actually keep. Sometimes you just want to be comfortable, and it's okay if that means wearing ugly pajamas.

● Am I your most difficult client? ●

Every. Single. Person. that I work with thinks that they are difficult or the most difficult client that I have ever had. There's (almost) always a brief period of time when a client and I are working together for the first time that's a little awkward, because I need to get to know them, in order to help them find their style.

This requires me to decode what they tell me, their body language, and then factor in their body type and budget to determine what clothes I should select for them. If a client is having difficulty communicating or is more guarded, this process can be challenging for me. However, I always make sure that they are happy in the end, and they're always surprised at how much fun they had working with a personal stylist.

● Being self deprecating is just talking ●
shit on yourself.

I don't care if it's "a joke," I don't let my friends say negative things about themselves, especially their bodies. The more time you spend with me (whether you're just reading this book, following me on social media, or hanging out), the more you will become kinder to yourself. It doesn't mean that you have to love everything about yourself all the time, because for some of us, that might feel unattainable. However, stop being mean to yourself. Would you want your best friend, partner, or child to say those kinds of things to themself? Then don't say it to yourself either.

Also, when you receive a compliment, if it's hard for you to hear it, practice just saying "thank you" and nothing else. There's a great Amy Schumer sketch that really highlights how much women struggle with just receiving compliments. We feel the need to justify it or put ourselves down, instead of just saying "thank you," and allowing the compliment to resonate in our bodies (if we so choose to).

The more that you just practice saying "thank you" after a compliment, the less you'll feel uncomfortable. It takes time, but you'll get there.

● Where do you shop for clients? ●

I get this question A LOT because people are curious! Honestly, it depends on the client! Where we shop varies depending on their personality, what they need, what they like, what part of their style journey they are currently on and where I want to take them.

I tell my clients all the time that they need to feel good in what they're wearing. When it comes to the decision making part of our time together, my opinion doesn't matter; their opinion does.

I could absolutely love something on you, but if you don't love it, you're not going to radiate confidence when you wear it. In fact, you'll probably never wear it. So, what's the point of cleaning out your closet of clothes that don't feel like you? Just to add new clothes that don't feel like you. It's silly, and I wouldn't be doing my job.

But Susan, you didn't answer my question! What kind of confession is this? Ok, you really want to know? I shop at Nordstrom, Bloomingdale's, Net-a-porter, Moda Operandi, Club Monaco, J-Crew, Express, Zara, Ann Taylor, Loft, The Real Real, thredUP, ASOS, local boutiques, independent designers, thrift stores, secondhand and consignment stores, and so many other places.

● Where do **you** shop? ●

Over time, I have been trying to become more aware of my consumption of fast fashion and make a stronger effort to support small businesses over large businesses, especially when it comes to my own personal shopping. Lately, I have been primarily shopping secondhand or small businesses, as well as designers who have values that I also want to support.

● Yes, I have my own style, and yes, it ● changes depending on the day

My style varies depending on my mood. When I am meeting with clients, or I have other appointments as a stylist, I like to look the part. I make sure that I am confident in what I am wearing, and my outfit shows that I am a personal stylist. I really enjoy mixing different styles rather than having one specific look. I also love that my tattoos help with that. I could wear an outfit that is super feminine and delicate, but with my tattoos exposed, my appearance is totally different than someone without a half sleeve.

I love bright patterns, heather gray, neon, black, pink, pleats, ruffles, studs, embroidery, sequins, leather, suede, vegan variations, laser cut, polka dots, modern, vintage, edgy, feminine, grunge, dresses, skinny jeans, skirts, distressed, boyfriend jeans, loafers, stilettos, sandals, boots, polished, funky, classic, and there's probably even more that I'm leaving out. My point is, I enjoy all of it. You'll see me wearing all of it (not at the same time). It all reflects me.

You don't have to pigeonhole yourself into a specific style genre, just like you don't have to only like one type of food. Some days, all I want is a cheeseburger and fries, and other days I eat overnight oats and vegan stir fry. Be in tune with yourself, and allow your style to be an extension of who you are and how you're feeling.

That being said, if you feel like shit, don't dress like shit.

Stylist tip: dress up a little when you have to go out and you're not feeling great (emotionally or physically). It will actually help improve how you feel. You'll stand taller, and throughout the day, you'll feel better. Trust me, try it. If there's one thing that we've all learned from being housebound for months with COVID-19, it's that putting on a little bit of makeup or cute clothes can truly lift your spirits. Even if I'm not feeling physically or emotionally great, and all I want to do is wear pants without buttons and a comfy shirt, I will still put on a little bit of makeup to differentiate between wearing pajamas and trying to function a bit better.

Q&A

What advice would you give clients who are looking to hire a stylist?

Channel your inner Scorpio/detective and do your research. Check out their website and their social media. Make sure that their personality and values align with yours. A stylist is someone who you will spend a lot of time with, and you will need to feel comfortable being vulnerable with them. If you can't let your guard down around them, the relationship won't be successful.

Shadow Side Shadow Side Shadow Side Shadow Side

ME AND MY SHADOW:
IT'S NOT ALL
"LOVE AND LIGHT"

Your shadow is always with you. There's no escaping it. Really, you have two ways of looking at it - the darkness you can't escape or the darkness that accompanies you to balance the light. I personally prefer the latter. Your shadow is part of you. You'll always have one.

Your shadow side refers to the parts of you that need your attention. When you choose to ignore your shadow side, you stop growing. You become emotionally stagnant.

You have to show up to be seen, but you don't need to be witnessed in order to transform. Your transformation happens on your own, but sometimes it takes something like a photograph in order for you to see yourself.

We're all growing and evolving at different stages of our lives. Allow it to happen. Witness the bravery and playfulness you had as a child and carry it with you to adulthood.

A transformation truly happens when you allow what's already inside of you to emerge. You discover it (or rediscover it) and fucking own it.

For me, it was my courage.

When I was six years old, my family and I vacationed at a dude ranch outside of Durango, Colorado. The first full day that we were at the ranch, we were introduced to our horses for the week. Just about every day that we were there, we went on a trail ride, so we spent a lot of quality time with our horses. I still remember very clearly thinking, "that can't be my horse, it's too big. I'm too small for that horse. Oh fuck, that's my horse. Okay, here we go. Let's do this." (Or ya know, the "six year old Susan" version of that. Six year old Susan didn't say "fuck"...11 year old Susan, now that's a different story.)

Riding that huge horse all over the mountains in Colorado for an entire week was an empowering experience, even as a six year old. I remember for years after that trip, my mom would remind me when I was feeling shy, and say things like, "Come on! You rode that giant horse like it was nothing, but you can't order your own ice cream?" Talking to strangers intimidated the shit out of me. Talking in front of people was terrifying. It always took me a long time to feel comfortable in order to open up to someone new. I was afraid of people. What would I do if they didn't like me? What if they judged me?

So instead of opening up to people, I protected myself by deflecting. I directed the conversation away from me by asking about them, insteading of sharing about myself. I still do this sometimes (I'm a Scorpio sun), but those closest to me know I'll open up and share when I'm ready. After working with middle school students for several years, I'm pretty sure that I can talk to just about anyone.

And I've stopped putting so much weight on the opinions of others (just remind me of that when I'm reading the reviews for this book). There are very few people more judgmental and intimidating than middle school girls. So, if I could release attachment to their opinions, I could release attachment to other people too.

The courage of a six year old on a giant horse trail riding in the mountains persevered when I needed to be confident in my own identity.

> Rediscovering my courage is a
> lesson that repeats for me.

Each time the lesson appears, it's different.

⇨ Making new friends/opening up to people
⇨ Ordering my own food
⇨ Performing on stage in college (playing the flute)
⇨ Co-creating a student run organization spreading awareness about domestic violence
⇨ Performing in The Vagina Monologues in college
⇨ Putting on concerts for the different ensembles that I conducted as a teacher
⇨ Becoming a mom
⇨ Leaving teaching
⇨ Creating my own business
⇨ Speaking for large events
⇨ Co-hosting all day workshops
⇨ Creating online courses, workshops, challenges

The weight of it changes. Sometimes the emphasis in being strong for myself, and other times it's the strength needed to show up for others. Now I see that these lessons keep reappearing, so that I can help more and more people rediscover their courage too.

I think it's really important to revisit positive memories that impacted who we are now. It's easy to get caught in a feedback loop of negative memories. We can get stuck, and feel like the trauma keeps happening, even after it's over.

But what if we tried to allow ourselves to mentally play in happy memories instead? When was a time in your life that you pleasantly surprised yourself by how brave or strong you were? How did that memory impact you in the future? How did that memory from your past self, high-five your present self and whisper, "you can do this?"

I'm loving this latest transformation of myself, and I can't wait for the next one.

Q&A

Do you have any advice for your
younger self?

Don't be afraid to be who you are. People may
not fully understand you, but the right people
will.

TRANSFORMATION

WHERE ARE THE STYLISH MOMS?: MOM ISN'T YOUR ONLY IDENTITY

Transformation Transformation Transformation

A few years ago, a friend sent me an article from Philly Mag. Being a stylist, friends and family often send me fashion related articles. The author of the Philly Mag article was a new mom, and she wrote about how her former life clothes no longer worked with her new mom lifestyle.

I immediately felt a connection with her article. I remember going through all of the phases of new mom attire. The first phase being, "leaving the hospital-what the fuck do I do with my body now that it's no longer housing a baby-no one warned me about this shit" outfits. Those included loose tops and pants that were basically leggings (okay, who are we kidding, they were maternity leggings).

My first "big" solo excursion out of the house without the bébé was the first time I was asked by a stranger when I was due and I told the woman, "3 weeks ago. My baby is with my mom, but thanks." And then I tried not to cry while waiting in line for lobster tails and other yummy pastries at Carlo's Bakery. She was standing in line with me, so, as awkward as you think it was, you're right.

That phase continued for the first 4ish months. Towards the end of that time, I moved into the second phase of new mom style, and finally accepted pants with a button and a zipper back into my life. Since I was home with Honey Bunny for the first 10 months, I wanted clothes that worked well while I was sitting on the floor with him. Most of my outfits were not accessorized because a lot of baby naps happened while I was holding him. Then as he got older, I didn't want him getting grabby with my earrings.

It wasn't until I went back to work that I felt like I was able to start dressing like "myself" again. That meant wearing clothes that could be "dry clean only," outfits that were fully accessorized, and shoes that had heels. Just like the author of the Philly Mag article, I had a closet of pieces I LOVED, but a lot of them didn't fit my post baby bod. Not to mention, so many of them were impractical for my new life as a mom.

Even before becoming a personal stylist, I was always stylish. I had a wide range of machine washable and dry clean only clothes. Clothing care directions and fit aside, some pieces were just out of the question, because I now had a baby to take care of.

When I was in the third stage of new mom style, aka the "back to work stage," every time I got dressed, I would see my clothes hanging there, and they reminded me that my body was different now. They were a reminder every day of what my body wasn't, and was never going to be again. Some people get back to their pre baby weight/body; I am not one of them, and after a lot of ongoing inner/ emotional work, I'm okay with that now.

As my son continues to get older, the activities we do together evolve. With his developing independence, my need to dress for his specific, chosen, activity occurs less. I can be outside to play with him, but I don't have to be sitting or crawling on the grass with him (unless I want to).

I have also curated clothes that are versatile, and have flexibility within my lifestyle as a mom, wife, personal stylist, and 30something year old who is occasionally not antisocial. So, over the years that I have been a mom, my personal style has evolved quite a bit. A lot of that has to do with my personal evolution. I'm constantly working on myself, doing "inner work," and that shows in my personal style.

Unfortunately, I often see that a lot of moms don't have that evolution of personal style. Once they become a mom, they lose their sense of self. Now, I'm not quite sure at what point in motherhood it develops for moms, but at some point after having a child the "mom disconnect" happens. I am convinced that there is something ingrained in us, as moms, that says, "If I dress in sweatpants or leggings or some form of athletic attire, it shows the world how hard I work." or "If I put a lot of effort in getting dressed, doing my hair, putting makeup on, I'm not the best mom that I can be."

Moment of truth: NONE of that is true.

There is so much pressure, as a mom to put your family first, to put your child's needs above your own. Of course it's natural to want to put their needs before yours, but you have to take care of yourself too. Remember, put your own oxygen mask on first, before assisting others. You can't pour from an empty cup.

Whatever Pinterest worthy quote you need to hear to understand the fact that you need to take care of your damn self in order to be your best self.

Of course there will be some days when leggings get the job done. You're at home, doing laundry, cleaning the house, doing food prep, working out, whatever kind of "at home" activity that day entails, you might need to wear leggings. No judgement here. I just don't want you to feel like every day needs to be a leggings day. Not every moment needs to be glamorous either. Balance can be achieved, even through the chaos of being a mom.

You need the RIGHT clothes, and I'm not talking about leggings and shapeless sacks. To share one example, get a good pair of jeans that have some stretch to them! This way, they will work with your post baby body, and then they will still fit well after your body continues to change. Dresses are also fantastic because they're one piece, so you don't need to think too much about how to put that outfit together. A dress with a defined, elastic waistband, and an A-line skirt is also very flexible, while your body is changing.

Also, find ways to make your life easier, so that you can dress well. It's completely acceptable to have an "I have lots of time" vs "I have a minute, maybe less" hair/makeup routine. A dress or jumpsuit that doesn't wrinkle is perfect for your "I have a minute" mornings.

When my son was younger, people who I had met were shocked to hear that I am a mom. Their reasons? Because my hair and makeup looked nice, and I was dressed in an outfit that is stylish. While I appreciate that these people were trying to give me a compliment, and had the best of intentions, I have made it my mission, as a personal stylist to remove the "moms should look sloppy or haggard" stigma.

What hurts my little stylist heart is hearing other women, other moms judge and shame each other for the way they look or dress. If you feel that's what I'm doing in this chapter, then

Go. Back. And. Read. Again.

I want to empower moms to get to know themselves again. You've changed since you became a mom. You've changed since you survived those first few days, months, years with your little one. Get to know yourself. Then let other people get to know you too, separate from the you that's a mom.

Express that new you through your personal style, and enjoy it.

Q&A

How do you define your personal responsibility as a stylist?

It is my personal responsibility to help my clients to discover who they want to be, what they want from their lives, how they want to show up, how they want to be seen, and help them to absolutely LOVE how they see themselves, and guide them towards achieving all of those goals.

WHAT TO WEAR WHEN YOU...: OH SHIT! I HAVE TO LOOK PRESENTABLE?

Transformation Transformation Transformation

Even after spending 12 months inside, I am sure that there are still days where you probably just want to wear sweatpants, leggings, or something with an elastic waistband. We all have days like that. On a cold, rainy weekend, even Honey Bunny doesn't want to get out of his pajamas.

So, when you have those "oh damn! I can leave my house again" moments, and you need to be somewhere where that kind of attire isn't acceptable, what do you do? That's where you need reliable pieces in your closet.

You need outfits that are for when you're thinking:

⇨   "I don't want to leave my house, but I have to."
⇨   "My stomach is more distended/bloated than it was when I bought those pants, I need a backup plan."
⇨   "I want to look like a strong, confident boss."
⇨   "Oh my gosh I don't have time to shave my legs or iron anything right now! I just need to get out the door and still look professional!"
⇨   "Let's show off this gorgeous bod!"

Why is it important to have outfits that check those boxes? Because you're busy, you're human, sometimes you oversleep, or you're running late, and you want your wardrobe to support you even in those moments. If your wardrobe supports you, then you will always want to get dressed looking like your best self, without needing to invest in a ton of time and effort. Isn't that the dream?

Let's give some examples of those kinds of outfits, shall we?

⇨ "I don't want to leave my house, but I have to".

    ⇨ Soft fabrics that resemble pajamas without looking like them.

    ⇨ Accessories that can make even a basic t-shirt look cool.

    ⇨ Comfortable shoes that have some detail to them that makes them look slightly elevated.

⇨ "My stomach is more distended/bloated than it was when I bought those pants, I need a backup plan."

    ⇨ Who says you have to wear pants? Dresses are great for days like these!

    ⇨ If you feel obligated to wear pants, joggers (sweatpants' fancier/bougier cousin) are a great alternative.

    ⇨ Wear a cool pair of earrings, a necklace, or scarf, and that will bring the visual attention up and away from your angry tummy.

⇨ "I want to look like a strong, confident boss."

    ⇨ This is when you need a dress or a jumpsuit that makes you feel like you can conquer the world. A one-piece outfit like a dress or a jumpsuit is also super easy - you don't need to add any other clothes to it to make it look complete and fierce. Choose your shoes and accessories, and you are done!

⇨ "Oh my gosh I don't have time to shave my legs or iron anything right now! I just need to get out the door and still look professional!"

    ⇨ A pair of pants that are dry clean only, and are made out of a material that you can wear all year. Why should they specifically be dry clean only? Great question. When you receive something back from the dry cleaners, they are already pressed, clean, and ready to go! There's usually little to no wrinkles, so it makes things easy to just grab and go.

⇨ "Let's show off this gorgeous bod!"

⇨ Babe, whatever makes you feel gorgeous, own it! Think about the parts of your body that you love, and highlight them! Stop focusing on what you want to hide, and shift that focus to what you want to highlight.

⇨ Also, practice saying, "Thank you," if you don't receive compliments well. When you wear something that makes you feel gorgeous, people will notice how you're feeling, so keep your chin up, and say "thank you."

> You need your clothes in your closet to support you and help you, not work against you. It's not just the special occasions in life that are important to shop for, but it's everything in between too.

If you're looking in your closet and feeling discouraged rather than inspired, you're missing out on a big part of your life.

We tend to put such a large emphasis on finding the perfect outfit for those special occasions and then just grab whatever is in your size for everyday clothes, but the logic there seems to be missing. Those "in between" moments are the life you're living every day.

Shouldn't the clothes that you need for your day to day life take precedence?

Give yourself permission to make yourself a priority.

What's your go-to look to celebrate your personal power?

An outfit with a bold color and pattern that makes me feel strong and feminine, jewelry that highlights and embraces my spirituality and includes crystals, and shoes with a little heel.

WE DON'T DO "JUST OKAY" ANYMORE: YOU'RE BETTER THAN THAT

When I first start working with a client one-on-one, we go through their entire closet together. Inevitably, we come across pieces, where I ask them, "How do you feel about this?" and a lot of the time they respond with "eh, it's okay."

To which, I reply:

> "We don't do *just okay* anymore.
> You deserve to have a closet with pieces that you love, that make you feel SO good.
> *Just okay* isn't good enough anymore.
> You have better options."

Why is "just okay" not enough? Continuing to choose something that's "just okay" means that you're allowing yourself to settle. You are making the decision to put yourself last, to not even take the time to think about what you really want. You're getting dressed by looking at your clothes and thinking "it's clean, it fits, I'll wear it."

When you choose your outfits in this way, it's usually because you're not prioritizing yourself in other areas of your life too. Parents, caretakers, business owners/executives, people with chronic illness, you know that I am talking to you. You can feel that, right? It's alright. I'm not mad. I'm calling you out because I know that you deserve better.

Now before that voice in your head starts to fight with me about this, I'm going to stop it right there. Ego (aka voice in your head), now's not the time. They're reading my book, so they get to listen to me right now. Thanks.

Alright, it's time for you to ask yourself:

⇨ Why am I not a top priority in my own life?

⇨ What's above me on my list of priorities?

⇨ Why do I think I don't deserve to be at the top of the list? (After you answer that question, take three deep breaths to reconnect with your body, and consciously release what you wrote down.)

⇨ What is something that I can do to make me feel like a priority in my own life?

When you're still in the process of working through T/trauma, answering these questions can be extra challenging. Your ego may try to come through and answer for you. It may try to convince you that you're not deserving, you're not worthy, or you're not enough.

If this happens to you, especially while you're trying to respond to the questions I included in this section of the book, close your eyes, take a deep breath, and say to yourself, "I acknowledge my reaction, but I release it, and I am choosing to think differently." Then ask yourself the question again.

Being able to answer questions that surround making yourself a priority in your life is a big step towards elevating your life. Otherwise, you'll keep yourself low on your priority list, which leads to diminishing everything else that you want for yourself from life.

If you're not a priority for yourself, you won't get a better job, a loving relationship, a dream lifestyle, make more money, travel, feel healthy, or love yourself. Take a minute and note how triggering that feels for you right now. Then release that and let it go too.

> ## You and your life deserve so much more than "just okay."

Let's revisit the last question I had you ask yourself: What is something that I can do to make me feel like a priority in my own life?

I would like for you to keep in mind that it doesn't have to be a grand gesture to make yourself feel like more of a priority. It can be something like ordering what you actually want from the menu, rather than worrying about the cost or judgement from others. Sometimes even just freely voicing your opinion in a conversation can feel like a small win. Think about it. How often do you respond with "it's okay," when it's actually not. Or when someone offers to get you something, your reply is, "no, I'm okay."

For most of us, our default response is to say "it's/I'm okay," because we're afraid of ruffling feathers, being a nuisance, or just being viewed as yourself (and risking being judged for it).

When you stop choosing clothes that are "just okay," it has a ripple effect in the rest of your life. Because it's about the clothes, but it's also about so much more than that.

It's about choosing yourself.

You're making the time to focus on you, and what you want. It's such an expansive feeling. You give yourself the permission to show up as yourself, fully.

Instead of saying "it's okay," you start responding with what you want, and how you actually feel.

You stop settling, and you find your voice.

Q&A

What are your plans for the future?

My plans for the future involve creating new adventures with my family, expanding my business in ways that align with my personal growth, and connecting deeper with myself through travel and inner work.

AFTERWORD: A MOTHER'S TALE DURING COVID (UPDATED)

Transformation Transformation Transformation

Editor's Note: A version of this piece was originally published in *Furious Lit vol. 1: Tell me a story*, Aug. 2020.

● Part One: Before ●

In the beginning of March, I was a badass business owner. I was in that state that every entrepreneur lives for, where you are just in the flow. Your constant hard work is now visible, you're working with your ideal clients, you feel like there's some kind of balance in your life, and things are just good.

I was also preparing to take my 5 year old son to Disney World for the first time. So, I am not a Disney person. If it weren't for my son, I would have absolutely no desire to be around anything Disney related whatsoever. It's just never been my thing. But, my inlaws offered to take all of us to Disney, and we knew that our little guy would love it.

A few days before we left, I remember my parents asking me, concerned, "Are you guys still going to Disney?"

"Yeah, why? There are no travel restrictions to Florida on the CDC website. We'll wash our hands like responsible adults, and I'm sure we'll be fine." I really didn't think we had any reason to be overly concerned, let alone stay home.

I told my son to be prepared that he may see people wearing

masks while we were in the airport, explaining to him that there is a virus, and we have to be extra thorough with washing our hands. So, that's exactly what we did.

We arrived at Disney World on Wednesday, March 11th, and everything seemed normal. We did the things you do at Disney – rides, food, all that Disney stuff.

My sister-in-law and her fiancé, who were also on the trip with us, were checking Twitter compulsively for updates. The frequency of their Twitter checks would increase progressively as our trip continued. Their stress induced (also inducing) Twitter scrolling was somewhat valid. By the second day of our trip, Thursday, March 12th, Disney announced that they would be closing the park Sunday night.

That's when shit got real. We changed our flight, so that we could leave Monday morning, instead of Wednesday. Disney added hand sanitizing stations throughout the parks. But, aside from the constant rising cases of COVID-19 being announced all over the world, "The Happiest Place on Earth" remained in its happy bubble, and wow, that felt strange.

Every time a notification went off on my phone, it was a client requesting to cancel, or an event I was invited to host that needed to be rescheduled. Remember that amazing flow state I mentioned earlier? I felt like the wave I was riding was crashing down. I'd say that's probably an accurate time stamp for when my depression started and my anxiety began to climb.

The last night that we were in Disney World, we were leaving Epcot at the end of the night, when the park was closing. This was the last night that Disney World would be open for an unknown length of time. The exit walkway was lined with Disney "cast members" all smiling and waving goodbye to all of us, as we filed out to the monorail and parking lot. I remember thinking, how many of these people will be affected by this virus? How many of them will get sick, die, or lose a loved one? Their behavior seemed so normal and "Disney-like." Was it because they wanted to try to spread hope, or were they keeping us in that protective Disney bubble?

We got home from Disney, and I think I was in some combination of shock and denial. My husband and I agreed to keep our son home, even though his school remained open for quite some time. I shifted from badass business working mom, to full time, stay-at-home mom, and that shift felt like crashing into a brick fucking wall. I don't remember when exactly, but the initial feelings of shock and denial transitioned quickly into grief. I was mourning the loss of my business, and the freedom from, what felt like, my past life.

● Part Two: During ●

Going from working mom to stay-at-home mom during a quarantine felt very similar to postpartum –you're at home, away from adults, your partner works all day (you used to work all day), and your needs take a back seat to that little human you created. Your emotions are on a roller coaster, and screaming isn't really an option.

Let's take a brief detour to discuss mental health, shall we? For the last 4+ years, I have been on medication to help manage my lifelong battle with anxiety and panic attacks. I have a regular spiritual practice, which includes meditation, sound healing, chakra balancing, energy clearing, journaling, mindfulness, and constant mindset work. I have worked with therapists. I have spiritual mentors. Before the quarantine, I was doing yoga regularly, and receiving both acupuncture and reiki.

I take care of myself.

I consider myself to be adaptable, optimistic, grounded, and strong, but a global trauma is not something anyone could have mentally or emotionally prepared for. Anxiety is being triggered in ways that seem new and old at the same time, and yet, none of my previous skills/tools/etc seem to be doing a damn thing.

Your detour has ended. You may now resume your original route.

I was forced to stop working for multiple reasons. The first reason was for our son's safety. With public schools closing all around us, we wanted to keep him home, despite his private daycare remaining open. The additional reasons happened quickly, so I don't remember the order they occurred, but basically, clients were cancelling, stores were being forced to close, malls shut down, and my business wasn't considered "essential."

Of course, a personal stylist is not essential. I get that. But, it's a strange feeling to hear that your business isn't "essential." I absolutely understand it from a logical perspective, but, when your business receives the unofficial title of "non-essential," it can bring your thoughts to dark places, especially if you are the one who created said business. It's like you and your business both got a huge punch in the emotional gut.

So, what did I do? I stopped. I stopped trying to work, to create, and I tried to be the best stay-at-home mom that I could be. You better believe I made a homeschool schedule that included school work, creative play time, outside time, and whatever else I'm sure you saw on those pictures that your friends posted on social media of the schedules they created for their kids.

And that lasted for a couple of weeks. What happened was, eventually, both my son and I hated the schedule. I was bored with it, and I knew that if I disliked it that much, my little guy hated it even more. I would go to bed at night, anxious about the next day. My nerves were fried. I felt resentful towards my husband, because he was still working, and thus able to leave the house, have his own thoughts, make decisions for himself, and listen to podcasts (oh, how I missed podcasts). I immediately felt guilty about having any kind of resentment towards my husband, because he really is an incredible human and partner, and then I became worried for his safety. And then I felt like an asshole. So, I cried a lot, and knew that something about my daily life had to change.

● Part Three: During, but Later ●

My friend and fellow creative, Stacey Fay, sent me a message pretty early on in the quarantine, telling me that she had an idea, and asked if we could chat on Zoom about it. She gave me a brief description of her idea, and I eagerly awaited our call. This call resulted in the birth of our video series and podcast, "The Creative Pause."

Up until this moment, I had been dealing with only uncertainty both in my business and my life. So when Stacey suggested creating something together, it felt like we were being guided to help people (and ourselves) in a way that we all desperately needed. It was crucial for us to provide a space for people to connect, whether the connection was literal, by joining in the show live, or emotional through a connection with what was shared in the show. The other key element to "The Creative Pause" involved encouraging our audience to take a little bit of time each day to do something that brings them joy. Connection and joy were two of the main pieces that both Stacey and I were missing in our lives. We needed it just as much as we wanted to provide it for our audience.

So many of our guests on "The Creative Pause" shared the message that there is beauty through imperfection, especially when you are in the creative process. I don't know that I ever really connected with being a perfectionist, but what I realized is that the fear of imperfection prevented me from trying a lot of new things. Hearing the message of "beauty through imperfection" over and over again eventually guided me to doing things like flower pressing, watercolor painting, lettering, cooking, baking, and establishing deeper connections with myself, nature, and my spirituality.

I am still trying to see all of the lessons that I have learned from being in quarantine; what are the elements of my new life that I am looking forward to taking with me, when our days have more flexibility?

I want to continue to support small and local businesses over big businesses, but no longer from a fear that they need my support, but because I want to help. I want to make the time to be able to prepare and cook the majority of our family meals, so we can be nourished with good food and love. Cooking has also become a creative outlet, and I would like to continue to create in the other ways that I have incorporated into my life. Quality alone time is something that I need to function at my best self. Spending time being surrounded by nature is also a necessity for me to recharge. These are beyond self care for me; it's what I need to help my mental health. At the same time, I need quality time being present with those I love.

Thinking about the future still makes me anxious. All of the unknowns and uncertainty stress me out, for sure. I'm going to try to shift my focus away from fear. I want to bring joy and connection to my life every day, and continue to help others find it too.

● Update 2021 ●

Reflecting back on a year is a tough process when that year didn't contain a global pandemic. While there were so many challenging aspects to it, there were also a significant amount of breakthroughs, both at a personal and global level.

As I'm writing this section, I am currently on an airplane.

AN AIRPLANE!

I'm fully vaccinated, and I am on my first flight in over a year. While one of my many goals for this book was to write content that was evergreen, I absolutely hope that this paragraph/section becomes outdated sooner rather than later.

But let's back up a little bit, shall we?

Sharing my experience and emotions about the first few months of the shut down was more healing than I ever anticipated. Writing it all down and publishing my story allowed me to have conversations with so many people who felt a connection to my experiences. When we would talk, we would both feel seen, heard, and understood.

One of the most important conversations that I had was with my husband, Tony. After writing the first part of this story, I realized that I had a lot of sadness that was presenting as anger and resentment. I was trying so hard to make the abrupt shift into full-time stay at home mom that I wasn't talking to Tony about how I felt about all of it.

I wanted it to look easy.

Hell, I desperately wanted it to be easy, or even just manageable, but it wasn't. I was constantly struggling, and felt obligated to just figure it out on my own. No one made me feel like I had to do it myself; it was just one of those tough situations we place onto ourselves.

When Tony read "A Mother's Tale During COVID-19," he was shocked. He didn't know the extent of how much I had been struggling. We talked, and made a lot of changes to our relationship and our parenting dynamic. We created a more balanced schedule that allowed both of us to have individual quality time with Honey Bunny, time for both of us to work, and time for ourselves (as a couple and separately).

We had to make a lot of really hard decisions together, including school for Honey Bunny. At the time, every choice felt like the wrong one. Every parent we talked to seemed to be doing something different with their kid for childcare or school. Our families only wanted us to be safe, but with my job and Tony's job, continuing to stay in complete isolation from the rest of the world was no longer an option.

These hard decisions really came down to what was best for our family, our unit as the three of us. All of this has evolved into the two of us sitting down together every Sunday to talk through what our upcoming week looks like. We plan out who's handling pick up or drop off, dinner plans, and if there are any days we anticipate needing to work late. The resentment that used to appear is no longer an issue, because we're essentially starting each week with "What do you need this week, and how can I help?"

A huge lesson for me is another one of those ongoing life lessons: learning to ask for help. Whether it involves being honest with Tony, and asking for what I need from him or realizing that I need help in my business.

Over the summer in 2020, I hired a business coach. I've worked with business coaches at different points throughout my career, and I truly find it an incredible, leveling up experience each time. (If you've read self-help books or listened to podcasts for entrepreneurs, this next part won't surprise you.) I made the decision to hire a business coach when my business was at a total standstill. I wasn't making any money, and yet I knew it was the perfect time to spend the most amount of money I've ever spent on hiring a coach. Why? Because at this time, I knew I had to completely change the way I ran my business.

The world had changed dramatically in just a few months, and no one knew what "normal" was going to look like. So I hired an expert to help me work through it. I now work with clients one-on-one for extended periods of time, nurturing their growth, supporting their inner and outer transformations, and enjoying the relationships that develop during that time together. Working with the coach for three months helped me completely transform my business. She helped me to find the value in myself and my business, during a time when I felt lost and confused.

My business was growing and evolving, and I was trying to run it with the same systems and methods that I was using before.

What's that saying about the definition of insanity?

For me, it didn't feel like insanity, but it did feel like burnout. This was another earth rattling moment for me. I had definitely experienced burnout before, but it was when I was teaching, and I was unhappy. I associated burnout with being miserable. Burnout happens when you're doing too much. When you're not taking proper care of yourself, and you allow yourself to drop to a lower spot on your priority list.

When I hit burnout, my priority list was
1. My business and clients
2. My family
3. My friends
4. Probably some other things
5. Me.

Thankfully, I have very special people in my life who were able to explain to me what I was going through (in a gentle way). My dear friend and business mentor, Nicole, told me, "You need to hire people to help you."

It was one of those experiences where I had been saying that to myself (and ignoring it), and then hearing her say it finally got that light bulb to turn on. So that's what I did!

Then when I started to burnout again a few months later, Nicole told me again, "You need to hire someone to help you with that." So I hired another person for my team, and another, and another. And for now, I feel like my team is complete, but as my business expands and evolves, the needs for my team will too.

"The Creative Pause" has evolved too during this last year.

Stacey and I recorded 50 episodes of the video series. We decided to take some time away from recording, and shifted our energy to other ways of reaching people through the show. By the time this book is published, the latest endeavour of "The Creative Pause" will be announced, and we'll see where it goes next. Having the connection with Stacey, our guests, and audience and the time to explore creatively helped me continue to move forward during the hardest times of 2020.

Around the time that I finished working with my business coach, Dani McDonald reached out to me on Instagram. Dani found me while searching to add a wardrobe stylist to the Wild Woman Soulography Experience, a completely transformative, spiritual photo shoot.

Dani connects with each woman prior to their shoot several times, feeling into the different archetypes that make up her true persona. The archetypes include the wild woman, the queen, the warrior, the innocent, and so many others. There is a lot of energy work involved in guiding each woman through her individual journey. So, it was important for Dani to find a stylist who could help create the looks for each archetype, while also supporting each woman she photographs. We chatted over Zoom, and she told me all about the Wild Woman Soulography Experience, and I was immediately on board.

At the time of publication for this book, Dani and I have traveled all over the East coast and California for soulography shoots. My Sagittarius moon rising absolutely love that I get to travel to beautiful places and do what I love.

Being able to watch and support each woman that we photograph is such a magical experience.

Creating such unique looks for each woman to represent their different archetypes is like helping them play dress up in a way that feeds their soul as an adult: adorning them with powerful jewelry, crowns, gowns, armor, fur, or sometimes just allowing them to show off their naked body. There is an incredible balance of vulnerability and strength that comes through during the entire experience.

It's a gift that I am truly grateful for.

SOULOGRAPHY: FEATURING THE PHOTOS OF DANIELA MCDONALD

Transformation Transformation Transformation

Jenny: Martha's Vineyard, MA The Lover

Emily: Charleston, SC The Innocent

Kristina: Ojai, CA The Soft Warrior

Kristen: Joshua Tree, CA The Lover

Kara: Carpinteria, CA The Warrior

Juliet: Whitewater, CA The Sage

Keri: East Haddam, CT The Creator

Brooke: Adirondacks, NY The Sage

Tisse: Garrison, NY The Medicine Woman

Susan: Long Beach Island, NJ The High Priestess

For more information on Susan's work

ADDITIONAL RESOURCES

● Learn More ●

About Susan Padron, her work, and her resources https://susanpadronstylist.com/

● Connect with Susan ●

/SusanPadronstylist

/SusanPadronstylist

● Discover Susan Padron's ●
newest projects

⇨ The Creative Pause
https://www.thecreativepauseproject.com/

⇨ Wild Woman Soulography
https://danimcdonald.co/wild-woman-soulography-experience

Susan Padron is an intuitive personal stylist. Through energy work and visualization, Susan guides her clients to rediscover their confidence within, so that you can emerge as the person you've always wanted to be. Susan has styled hundreds of people all ranging in age from 7 to 80 years old, enjoying the process of highlighting their uniqueness through their personal style.

A Note to Our Furious Readers

From all of us at Read Furiously, we hope you enjoyed Susan Padron's style guide and spiritual memoir, *We don't do "just okay" anymore*.

There are countless narratives in this world and we would like to share as many of them as possible with our Furious Readers.

It is with this in mind that we pledge to donate a portion of these book sales to causes that are special to Read Furiously and the creators involved in *We don't do "just okay" anymore*. These causes are chosen with the intent to better the lives of others who are struggling to tell their own stories.

Reading is more than a passive activity – it is the opportunity to play an active role within our world. At Read Furiously, its editors and its creators wish to add an active voice to the world we all share because we believe any growth within the company is aimless if we can't also nurture positive change in our local and global communities. The causes we supportare culturally and socially conscious to encourage a sense of civic responsibility associated with the act of reading. Each cause has been researched thoroughly, discussed openly, and voted upon carefully by our team of Read Furiously editors.

To find out more about who, what, why, and where Read Furiously lends its support, please visit our website at readfuriously. com/charity

Happy reading and giving, Furious Readers!

Read Often, Read Well,
Read Furiously!

LOOK FOR THESE OTHER GREAT TITLES FROM

Read Furiously
Read Often. Read Well.

Poetry
All These Little Stars
Silk City Sparrow
Dear Terror
Whatever you Thought, Think Again
Until the Roof Lifted Off
Chocolate Brown Satin Hot Pants and Other Artifacts
Heirlooming

Essays and Anthologies
Nerd Traveler
Furious Lit vol 1: Tell Me A Story
The World Takes: Life in the Garden State
Putting Out: Essays on Otherness
Working Through This

The One 'n Done Series
Helium
Brethren Hollow
Girls, They'll Never Take Us Alive
What About Tuesday

Graphic Novels
Pursuit: A Collection of Artwork
In the Fallout
Brian & Bobbi
The MOTHER Principle

CPSIA information can be obtained
at www.ICGtesting.com
Printed in the USA
BVHW021331170921
616963BV00005B/19